2RES PZ 10.
acDonald,
phabatics

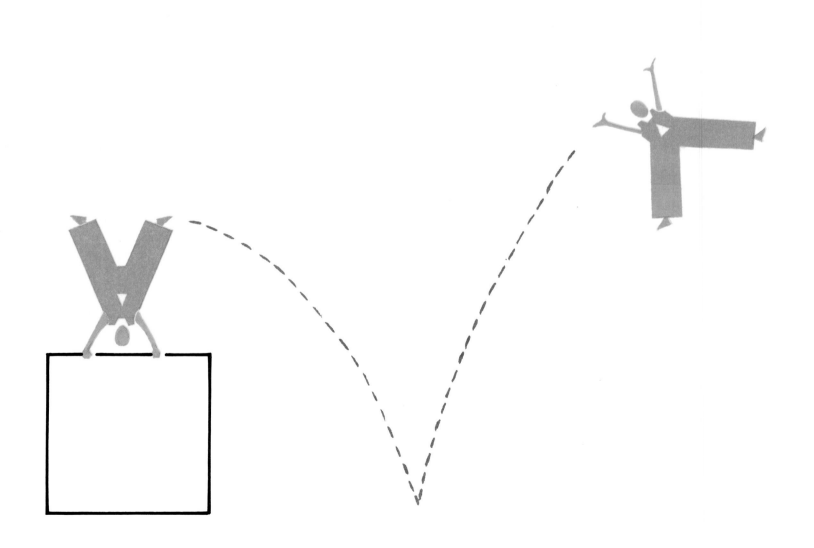

# ALPHABATICS

## Suse MacDonald

**HARCOURT BRACE & COMPANY**
Orlando   Atlanta   Austin   Boston   San Francisco   Chicago   Dallas   New York
Toronto   London

# Aa

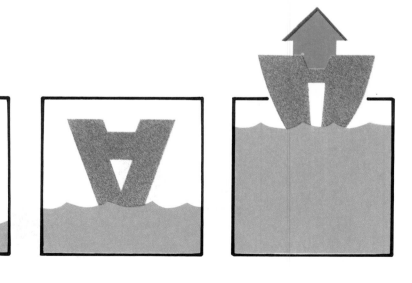

**Bb**

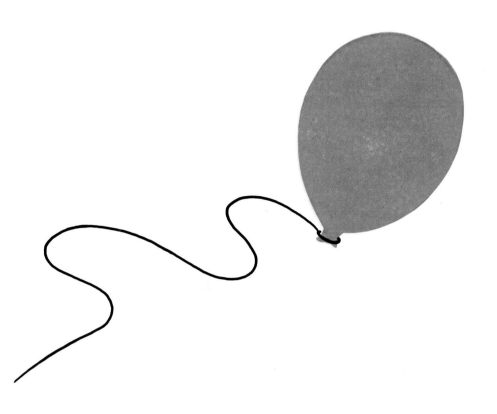

balloon

Cc

# Clown

# Dd

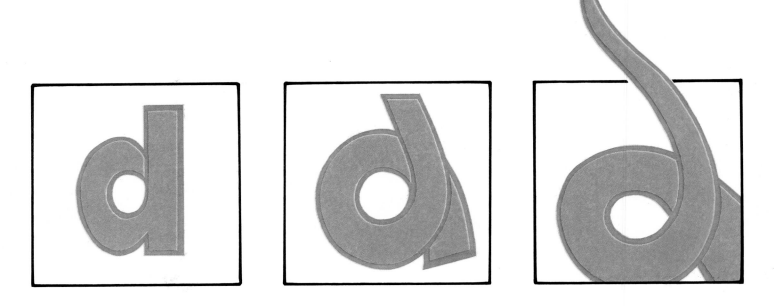

dragon

# Ee

# Ff

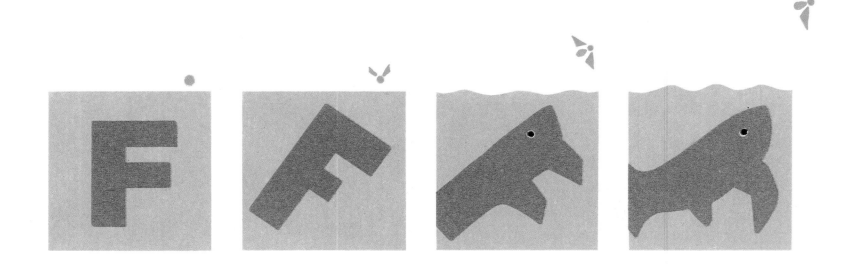

# Fish

# Gg

# Giraffe

Hh

house

**insect**

# Jj

**jack-in-the-box**

# Kk

K

Kite

# Ll

Lion

# Mm

mustache

# Nn

nest

# Oo

owl

**Plane**

# Qq

Quail

# Rr

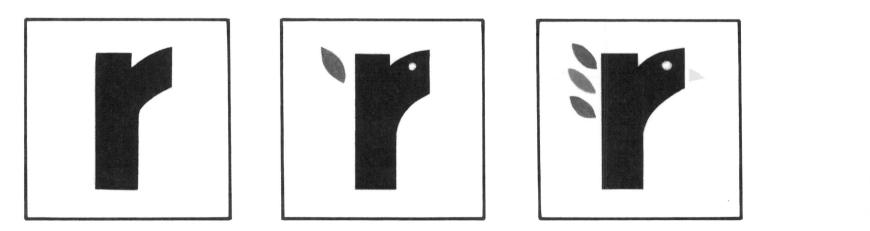

rooster

# Ss

# Swan

**Tt**

**Tree**

# Uu

**umbrella**

# Vv

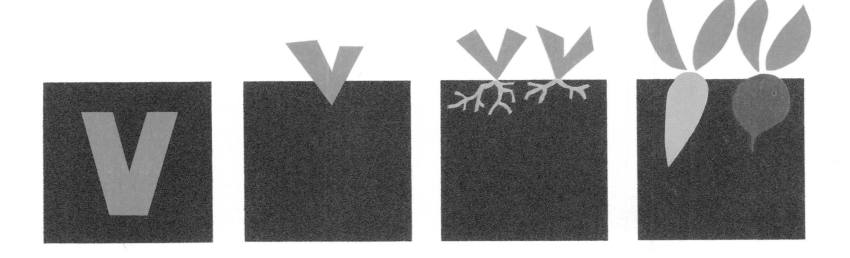

# Vegetables

# Ww

# Whale

# Xx

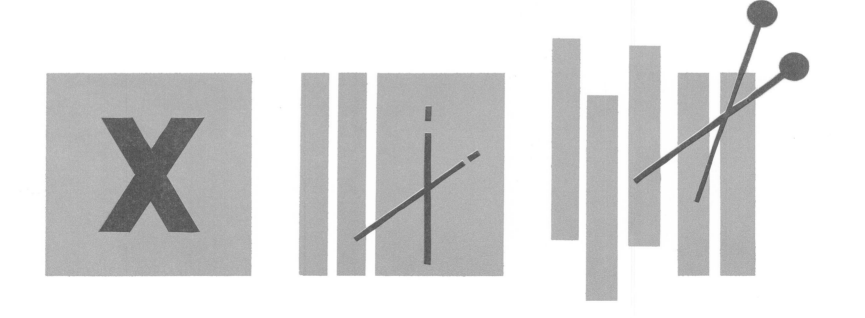

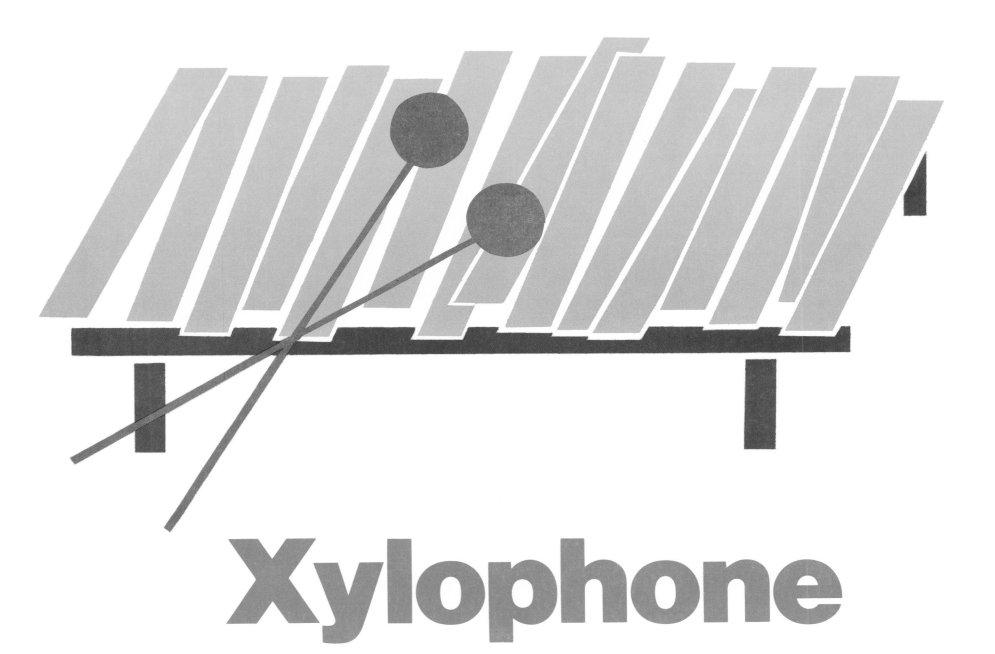

Xylophone

# Yy

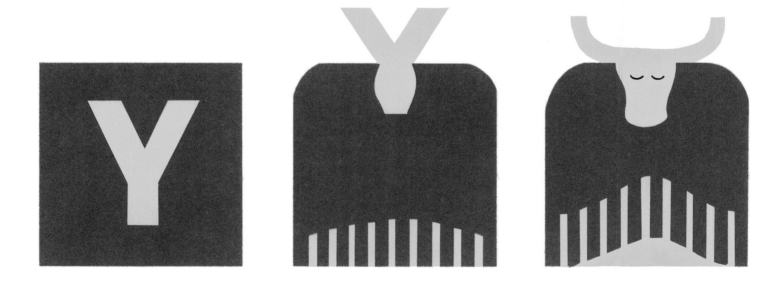

Yak

# Zz

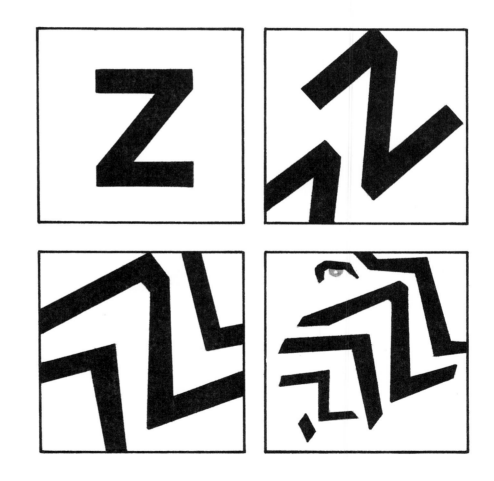

Zebra

**For Stuart, with special thanks to Susan and Deborah**

This edition is published by special arrangement with Bradbury Press, an Affiliate of Macmillan, Inc.

Grateful acknowledgment is made to Bradbury Press, an Affiliate of Macmillan, Inc. for permission to reprint *Alphabatics* by Suse MacDonald. Copyright © 1986 by Suse MacDonald.

Printed in the United States of America

ISBN 0-15-302107-1

2 3 4 5 6 7 8 9 10   035   97 96 95 94 93